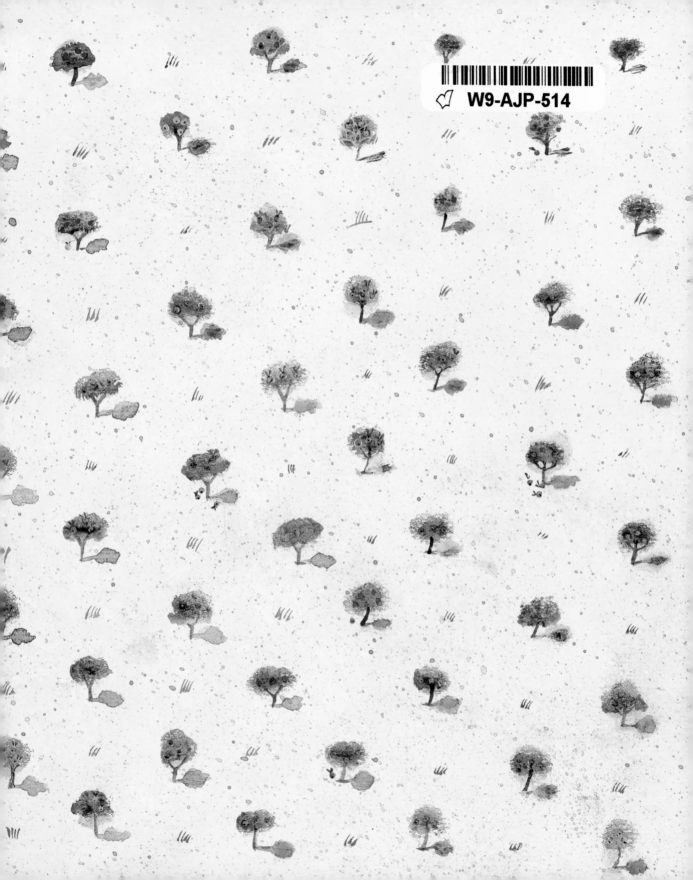

Published by Roaring Brook Press
Roaring Brook Press is a division of Holtzbrinck Publishing Holdings Limited Partnership
143 West Street, New Milford, Connecticut 06776
First published in Sweden in 2002 by Rabén & Sjögren Bokförlag, Stockholm

Distributed in Canada by H. B. Fenn and Company Ltd.

Library of Congress Cataloging-in-Publication Data
Näslund, Görel Kristina.
[Lilla appelboken. English]
Our Apple Tree/Görel Kristina Näslund; illustrated by Kristina Digman—1st American ed.
p. cm.
1. Apples–Life cycles–Juvenile literature. 2. Apples–Juvenile literature. I. Digman, Kristina,
ill. II. Title
SB363.N2713 2005   634'.11–dc22

2004022493

ISBN: 1-59643-052-4

Roaring Brook Press books are available for special promotions and premiums.
For details, contact: Director of Special Markets, Holtzbrinck Publishers.

First American Edition August 2005
Printed in the United States of America
10 9 8 7 6 5 4 3 2

Görel Kristina Näslund

Our Apple Tree

Illustrated by Kristina Digman

Roaring Brook Press
New Milford, Connecticut

All winter long,
our apple tree rests.

But not everyone is asleep.

Nuthatches look for little bugs under the tree's bark.

Pheasants and blackbirds eat last year's apples,
still lying frozen on the ground.

When spring comes, our apple tree wakes up.
Pink buds and white blossoms show that it is ready
to make apples again.

Bees come to visit, flying from blossom to blossom.

They visit every apple tree for miles around.

Every day the bees gather sweet nectar and dusty pollen.

Every night they go home to make honey
and feed their babies.

Wherever the bees go, they take
some pollen and leave some pollen
behind.

And soon the blossoms begin
to turn into the tiniest apples,
all soft and downy.

In the warm sun, the apples
grow bigger and bigger.

Our apple tree is hard
at work.

All summer long, all over the world, other apple trees
are growing apples, too. Some apples are golden.
Some are pink. Some have stripes. Some blush.

Every apple has a name of its own.

This kind is called Delicious.

Doesn't it look delicious?

Once you start eating an apple, it's hard to stop.
Crunch, crunch . . . you're at the core!
The seeds nestle inside.

Every seed could be an apple tree
like ours someday.

The apples are still growing
and ripening on our apple tree
and apple trees everywhere.
But soon, very soon,
it will be time to make
apple art . . .

. . . and applesauce

. . . and apple pie.

We could even have an apple party
for all our friends!

Everyone likes apples.

It's autumn! Our apple tree has a wonderful gift for us.
The apples are ripe! We'll pick some and eat some
and store some away.

As soon as the last apple is safe inside, cold winds begin to blow. The leaves fall from our tired apple tree.

And then it's time to rest again...
and dream of next year's apples.

Apple Crisp

Ingredients

Filling:

$1/2$ cup granulated sugar
1 tablespoon all-purpose flour
$1/2$ tablespoon cinnamon
$1/8$ teaspoon salt
8 cups sliced peeled apples

Topping:

1 cup all-purpose flour
1 cup rolled oats
1 cup packed brown sugar
$1/2$ teaspoon baking powder
$1/4$ teaspoon baking soda
$1/2$ cup butter, cut into small pieces

Directions

1. Preheat oven to 375 degrees F.
2. In mixing bowl, combine sugar, 1 tablespoon flour, cinnamon, and salt. Add apples and toss gently to coat. Spread apples in a 13 x 9 x 2-inch baking dish.
3. In bowl, combine 1 cup flour, oats, brown sugar, baking powder, and baking soda. Cut in butter pieces until clumps form. Sprinkle over apple mixture.
4. Bake, uncovered, in a 375 degree F oven 35 minutes or until bubbly and apples are tender. Serve when cool.

Makes 8 servings.